TOP TEN BIGGEST WONDERS ON EARTH

BY JOHN ALLAN

CONTENTS

WELCOME TO THE WORLD'S BIGGEST!	4
BIGGEST FOOD FIGHT	6
BIGGEST CAVE	8
BIGGEST AIRCRAFT	10
BIGGEST LAND ANIMAL	12
BIGGEST FLOWER	14
BIGGEST TREE	16
BIGGEST DESERT	18
BIGGEST WATERFALL	20
BIGGEST BUILDING	22
BIGGEST SEA ANIMAL	24
BIGGEST THING IN OUTER SPACE	26
CLOSE, BUT NOT CLOSE ENOUGH!	28
THE PEOPLE BEHIND THE RECORDS	30
GLOSSARY	31
INDEX	32

Copyright © 2025 Hungry Tomato Ltd

First published in 2025 by Hungry Tomato Ltd
F15, Old Bakery Studios, Blewetts Wharf, Malpas Road, Truro, Cornwall, TR1 1QH, UK.

No part of this publication may be reproduced, stored in a retrieval system, or transmitted in any form or by any means, electronic, mechanical, photocopying, recording, or otherwise, without prior written permission of the copyright owner.

A CIP catalogue record for this book is available from the British Library.

ISBN 9781835694213

Printed in China

Discover more at
www.hungrytomato.com

Words in **BOLD** can be found in the glossary.

WELCOME TO THE WORLD'S BIGGEST!

We live on a planet with so many impressive things. Prepare to be amazed by some of the world's biggest record-breakers...

MADE BY HUMANS OR NATURE?

The biggest things in the world come in all shapes and sizes. Some are incredible wonders of nature, from landscapes to animals, and others are incredible human-made machines.

MEASURING SIZE

You can usually see when something is big, but how can you tell exactly how big it is? Size is usually measured by working out the height, length, and width of something. From this, we can calculate its overall size. In the case of events, size is measured by the number of people attending.

MAKING HISTORY

We have found so many incredible record-breaking things on our planet, but there are still so many places we haven't explored yet. Modern technology is getting better all the time, so new things are being uncovered all the time by people whose names will go down in history!

HOLDING ONTO A RECORD

Humans are always hoping their creations will break records. People across the world are always competing to build bigger, better, and even more impressive structures to achieve these dreams. This means that records are constantly changing.

This book showcases 10 of the biggest things in the world!
It's hard to compare these record-breakers as they are all so different. What's big for an animal may seem tiny compared to a building, but it's still impressive. The top 10 in this book are in no particular order, but everyone will have a favourite!

1 BIGGEST FOOD FIGHT

On the last Wednesday of August, the biggest annual food fight takes place in Buñol, Spain. It's called La Tomatina, and it has been celebrated since 1945!

La Tomatina is a festival where people throw tomatoes at each other in the streets! More than 100,000 kilograms (22,000 lbs) of tomatoes are thrown in total. Around 20,000 people take part in the festival every year, with many of them visiting from all over the world to join in!

The tomato fight lasts for one hour exactly. After the fight has finished, fire engines hose people down!

DID YOU KNOW?

Only really **overripe** or rotting tomatoes are used because they're really soft, so they don't hurt people. This also means that La Tomatina is not wasting **edible** food.

SUPER FACT

Only about 9,500 people live in the town of Buñol normally, so La Tomatina almost triples the number of people, even if only for a few days!

2 BIGGEST CAVE

Hidden so deep in the jungle that it was only discovered in the 1990s, Vietnam's Hang Son Doong cave is the biggest cave in the world.

Hang Son Doong is 5 times bigger than the next biggest natural cave in the world. It's 5.5 miles (9km) long and has a volume of 38.5 million cubic metres. It's so big that it has rivers and lakes inside it, and it even experiences mist and clouds.

This 3-million-year-old cave has several natural skylights which let sunlight in, allowing plants to grow inside the cave! To protect the cave, only 1,000 visitors are allowed inside every year.

SUPER FACT

This cave is also famous for its huge "cave pearls"! These aren't real pearls – they are made of **minerals** that have dripped off the rock ceiling and formed spheres over a long period of time.

DID YOU KNOW?

Hang Son Doong is also home to some of the biggest **stalactites** and **stalagmites** in the world!

3 BIGGEST AIRCRAFT

It may look like two, but Stratolaunch is one plane. It's the biggest aircraft ever (by wingspan), stretching 117 metres (385 ft) from wingtip to wingtip – that's longer than a football pitch!

DID YOU KNOW?

Stratolaunch was designed to help launch satellites into outer space.

SATELLITE

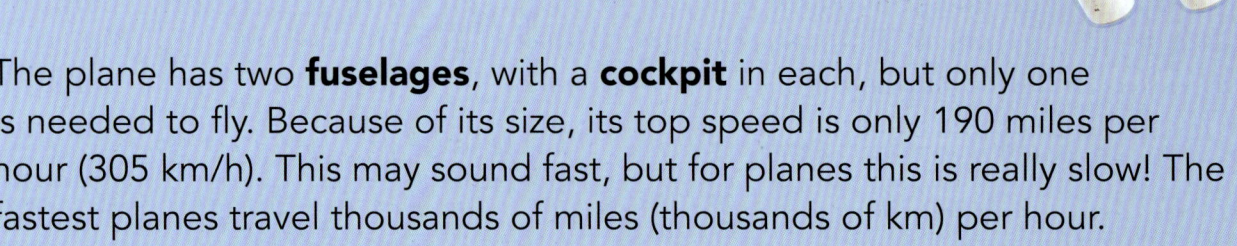

The plane has two **fuselages**, with a **cockpit** in each, but only one is needed to fly. Because of its size, its top speed is only 190 miles per hour (305 km/h). This may sound fast, but for planes this is really slow! The fastest planes travel thousands of miles (thousands of km) per hour.

This mighty machine took years to build. It was so big that an extra-large **hangar** had to be built especially so that the plane could be constructed and stored inside!

SUPER FACT

Stratolaunch is also called "Roc", after a gigantic legendary bird that was said to be big enough to pick up elephants!

4 BIGGEST LAND ANIMAL

The African bush elephant is the biggest animal on land. In fact, everything about this elephant is BIG!

This elephant can grow to be 9 metres (30 ft) long from trunk to tail and 4 metres (13 ft) tall. As well as being the biggest land animal, it is also the heaviest land animal living on Earth today!

To keep their huge bodies strong and healthy, elephants need to eat lots of food. African bush elephants eat about 150 kilograms (300 lbs) of food every day – that's the same weight as a sofa! This means they spend most of their day eating.

DID YOU KNOW?

Even their babies are big! Baby elephants are born a similar size to fully-grown panda bears.

SUPER FACT

Elephants' tusks are actually teeth! The longest recorded tusk was 3.5 metres (11.5 ft).

5 BIGGEST FLOWER

Growing in the rainforest is the enormous rafflesia arnoldi. It's the world's biggest flower, and one that you may want to stay away from...

Many people call the rafflesia arnoldi the smelliest flower in the world. It doesn't smell nice either – this red flower stinks of rotting meat, winning it the nickname "corpse flower"! It may not seem nice to us, but the smell attracts flies and beetles that help the flower spread its **pollen**.

This flower can grow to be more than 1 metre (3 ft). Unusually, it doesn't have any leaves, stems, or roots. It grows on other plants' bark and vines, instead and relies on their **nutrients** to grow.

DID YOU KNOW?

Once it has fully developed, the flower only lives for a few days!

SUPER FACT

This huge flower can weigh as much as 11 kilograms (24 lbs) – that's heavier than some dogs!

6 BIGGEST TREE

Stretching high and wide into the sky from the forests of California, USA, the General Sherman is the world's biggest living tree.

General Sherman is a giant sequoia tree that measures 84 metres (276 feet) tall. This makes it shorter than the world's tallest living tree – Hyperion, a Californian redwood tree – but because General Sherman's trunk is so thick, its overall size is much bigger!

General Sherman is thought to be around 2,200 years old. It grows by adding new wood to its trunk every year. Some people have estimated that, in one year, it grows enough extra wood to build a five or six-room house!

DID YOU KNOW?

It is estimated that there is enough wood in the General Sherman to make 5 billion matchsticks!

SUPER FACT

Some of General Sherman's branches are thicker than other types of trees' trunks!

7 BIGGEST DESERT

It may surprise you to find out that Antarctica is the largest desert in the world! It covers 5.5 million square miles (14.2 million square km); an area much bigger than the USA.

Deserts aren't always hot – Antarctica is freezing! But it counts as a desert because it gets hardly any rain each year. Antarctica holds most of the freshwater on Earth, but it's locked in as ice.

SUPER FACT
Antarctica is also the highest, driest, coldest, and windiest **continent** on Earth!

While most deserts only cover part of a continent, the Antarctic desert covers the whole continent of Antarctica. This frozen desert is almost double the size of the Sahara – the largest hot desert, and perhaps the most famous desert, in the world.

DID YOU KNOW?

Antarctica may be covered in ice now, but scientists think that 90 million years ago it was warm and covered in **tropical rainforest**!

8 BIGGEST WATERFALL

Considered one of the seven natural wonders of the world, Victoria Falls is also the biggest waterfall in the world!

This waterfall is so big that it spans two different countries! It's made up of five sections of waterfall; four are in Zimbabwe and one is in Zambia. It's not quite the tallest or widest in the world, but it's the world's largest sheet of falling water.

It's estimated that 500 million litres (110 million UK gallons) fall over Victoria Falls every minute. That's enough to fill 200 Olympic swimming pools. It's so loud that it can be heard many miles (km) away.

DID YOU KNOW?

Victoria Falls is twice as wide and twice as tall as Niagara Falls, located on the border between Canada and the USA.

NIAGARA FALLS

SUPER FACT

Victoria Falls isn't this waterfall's only name! It is often called "Mosi-oa-Tunya", which comes from a local language and means "the smoke that thunders".

9 BIGGEST BUILDING

The tallest human-made structure in the world is the Burj Khalifa, a skyscraper in Dubai, UAE.

This impressive building took 6 years to build. It stands 830 metres (2,700 ft) tall and is made up of more than 160 floors. It also holds the record for being the tallest free-standing structure, the highest outdoor observation deck, and more!

To be this tall, the building had to be carefully planned so that it could cope with extreme weather like strong winds. It is supported by thick concrete foundations and walls, and its structure has been designed to withstand earthquakes.

DID YOU KNOW?

The building is used by many different people; some of its floors are for people to live, some for people to work, and others for entertainment.

SUPER FACT
This huge building can hold up to 10,000 people at one time!

10 BIGGEST SEA ANIMAL

Not only is the blue whale the biggest sea animal, it's the biggest animal in the world, and the biggest animal that has ever lived – it's bigger than every dinosaur ever discovered.

These impressive creatures can grow up to 30 metres (10 ft) long and can weigh as much as 30 African bush elephants! Everything about these animals is huge: their hearts weigh the same as a motorbike, and their lungs hold 1,000 times more air than human lungs!

Blue whales have the biggest hearts of any living animal. They are huge because they need to pump lots of blood around the whales' bodies to keep them alive.

SUPER FACT
Blue whales hold the record for heaviest tongue in the world. Their tongues are usually the same weight as an elephant!

DID YOU KNOW?

Blue whales have to eat lots of food to power their big bodies. Scientists used to think they ate 4 tonnes (4.4 US tons) of krill per day, but estimates now suggest they eat up to four times that amount!

BIGGEST THING IN OUTER SPACE

You've now heard about 10 of the most incredibly big things in the world. But what about the biggest thing in outer space?

In our solar system, the biggest thing is the Sun. It's so big that you could fit 1.3 million Earths inside it! It's a burning ball of gas whose heat is so powerful that we can still feel it millions of miles (millions of km) away.

Our Sun is a big star, but it's not the biggest. The biggest star we have discovered so far in outer space is a supergiant called UY Scuti. It's so big that you could fit 5 billion of our Suns inside it!

SUPER FACT

The biggest structure in the universe isn't just a single thing – it's a collection of **galaxies** that span 10 billion **light-years** across! It's called The Hercules–Corona Borealis Great Wall.

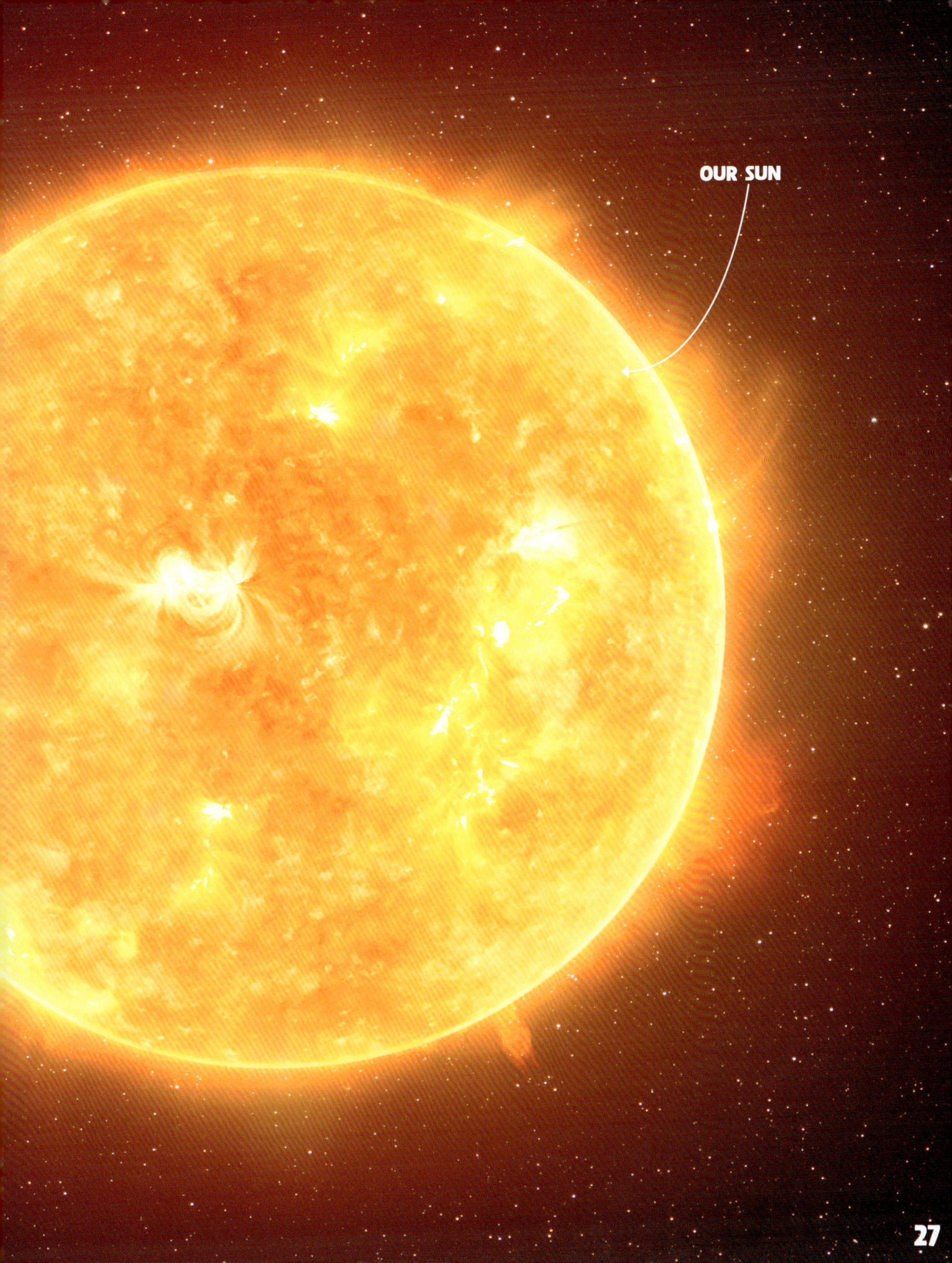

CLOSE, BUT NOT CLOSE ENOUGH!

There are lots of amazingly huge things on Earth that didn't quite make our top ten. Here are some impressive runners-up.

BIGGEST CRYSTALS

The biggest crystals ever discovered are in a place called the "Cave of the Crystals", which is in Mexico. They are around 11 metres (36 feet) long, which is the same length as a school bus!

BIGGEST LIVING STRUCTURE

The Great Barrier Reef in Australia is the biggest living structure in the world. It's made up of coral reefs which cover an area the size of Italy! It's home to thousands of different plants and animals.

BIGGEST FLYING ANIMAL

From **fossils**, scientists estimate that the wingspan of Quetzalcoatlus was 11-13 metres (36-42 ft), which makes it the biggest flying animal to ever exist! It lived alongside the dinosaurs about 70 million years ago.

BIGGEST ROCK

Mount Augustus in Australia is the biggest rock in the world! It's called "Burringurrah" by the local Wajarri community and stands 715 metres (2,350 ft) tall. Only the fittest hikers attempt to climb it!

BIGGEST DUMP TRUCK

The biggest dump truck ever created is the BelAZ 75710. This gigantic vehicle was designed to help move huge amounts of heavy material, like rock, in quarries and mines.

THE PEOPLE BEHIND THE RECORDS

Humans have discovered and created some incredible things throughout history. Here's just some of the people behind the amazing records in this book.

HO KHANH

In 1990, Ho Khanh made an incredible discovery – he found the world's biggest cave, Hang Son Doong, while on an expedition in the jungle. He now works as a cave guide, conservationist, and tour business owner.

LA TOMATINA

It's said that La Tomatina, the world's biggest food fight, first started when a food fight broke out between two groups of friends during a parade in the town. After that, it became a yearly tradition.

PAUL ALLEN & BURT RUTAN

In 2011, Microsoft co-founder, Paul Allen teamed up with Scaled Composites co-founder Burt Rutan to develop Stratolaunch – the world's biggest plane. They hoped their design would revolutionise space transport.

GLOSSARY

Annual – something that happens every year.

Cockpit – the small space inside an aircraft where the pilot sits and controls the plane.

Continent – one of the huge pieces of land on Earth. For example, Africa and North America are separate continents.

Edible – something that is safe to be eaten.

Fossils – the remains or impression of plants and animals that lived long ago.

Fuselage – the main body of an aircraft.

Galaxies – huge collections of gas, dust, and billions of stars and their solar systems, all held together by gravity.

Hangar – a covered, enclosed area for housing and repairing aircraft.

Light-years – a unit of distance that measures how far light travels in one year.

Minerals – substances that are naturally found in things like rocks, sand, and soil. Many minerals form as crystals.

Nutrients – substances or ingredients that plants and animals need to live and grow.

Overripe – when fruit becomes too ripe and goes past its best.

Pollen – a fine powder produced by some plants when they reproduce.

Stalactites – formations that are made from minerals, but that look like icicles and grow down from cave ceilings.

Stalagmites – formations that are made from minerals, but that look like icicles that are growing up from cave floors. They are usually underneath stalactites (see above).

Tropical rainforest – a forest that is very hot and wet, and the plants grow closely together. They are usually found near the equator.

INDEX

A
Allen, Paul 30
Antarctica 18-19

B
BelAZ 75710 (truck) 29
Blue whale 24-25
Burj Khalifa, UAE 22-23
Burringurrah (see: *Mount Augustus*)

C
Cave of the Crystals, Mexico 28

E
Elephants 11, 12-13, 24

G
General Sherman (tree) 16-17
Great Barrier Reef 28

H
Hang Son Doong, Vietnam 8-9, 30
Hercules–Corona Borealis Great Wall 26
Hyperion (tree) 16

K
Khanh, Ho 30

L
La Tomatina festival 6-7, 30

M
Microsoft 30
Mount Augustus, Australia 29

Q
Quetzalcoatlus 29

R
Rafflesia arnoldi 14-15
Rainforest 14-15, 19, 31
Roc (mythical bird) 11
Rutan, Burt 30

S
Satellite 10
Scaled Composites 30
Stratolaunch 10-11, 30
Sun 26-27

U
UY Scuti (star) 26

V
Victoria Falls, Zambia & Zimbabwe 20-21

Picture credits:
Abbreviations: m-middle, t-top, l-left, r-right, bg-background.

Wikipedia: By Alexander Van Driessche - Gaianauta received this from Alexander Van Driessche via Email., CC BY 3.0, https://commons.wikimedia.org/w/index.php?curid=23231964 28ml. Shutterstock: aappp 10ml; Ajit SN 4ml, 24-25bg; Andrew Linscott 1bg, 12-13bg; BearFotos 7bg, 30mr; Angel Dibello 10-12bg, 30bl; atgier 28br; ByDroneVideos 21bg; EcoPrint 12br; Ferdi Awed 14b; Gulf MG 3bg; Harmony Video Production 22br; Holiday.Photo.Top 16b; Independent birds 31br; Irina Starikova1811 6b; Jody Hinterleitner 18-19bg; kamomeen 29tl; Kid 315 8-9bg, 30tl; LeitWolf 29bl; Lukasz Pawel Szczepanski 26-27bg; marc witte 29mr; New Africa 4br; Sergii Figurnyi 20br; Stefano Borsa 17bg; Tarpan 25tr; Teo Tarras 19mr; TTStudio 5br, 23bg; Vietnam Stock Images 5tl, 9tr; Zulazhar 15bg.

Every effort has been made to trace the copyright holders, and we apologise in advance for any unintentional omissions. We would be pleased to insert the appropriate acknowledgements in any subsequent edition of this publication.